GW00496757

MICHAEL BALL

THE MAN WITH THE

GOLDEN VOICE

(A BIOGRAPHY)

AMANDA GERALDINE

All rights reserved. No part of this publication may be reproduced, distributed, or transmitted in any form or by any means, including photocopying, recording, or other electronic or mechanical methods, without the prior written permission of the publisher, except in the case of brief quotations embodied in critical reviews and certain other non-commercial uses permitted by copyright law.

Copyright © Amanda Geraldine, 2023.

Table Of Contents

Preface

Michael Ashley Ball OBE, an English singer, presenter, and actor, was born on June 27, 1962. He appeared in the 1985 West End premiere of Les Misérables in London as Marius Pontmercy before moving on to perform in The Phantom of the Opera in 1987 as Raoul. He performed the song "Love Changes Everything" from the musical Aspects of Love, where he played Alex, and it helped him climb to number two on the UK Singles Chart in 1989. Both in London and on Broadway, he performed the part. Coming Home To You, his fourth number-one album to date, peaked at number one in the UK. With

combined chart sales of 82,000, Ball and
Captain Tom Moore's cover of "You'll Never
Walk Alone" peaked at number one on the UK
Singles Chart on April 24, 2020, becoming the
year's fastest-selling song.

Ball participated in the 1992 Eurovision Song
Contest on behalf of the United Kingdom, and
his song "One Step Out of Time" placed
second. He played Marius once more in Les
Misérables: The Dream Cast in Concert in 1995.
His past West End performances include
Caractacus Potts in Chitty Chitty Bang Bang
(2002) and Giorgio in Passion (1997).

The Laurence Olivier Award for Best Actor in a Musical has been given to him twice. He first won in 2008 for his portrayal of Edna Turnblad in Hairspray. Then, in 2013, he won again for playing the main character in the revival of Sweeney Todd: The Demon Barber of Fleet Street.

As part of the 2015 Birthday Honors, Ball received the OBE designation for his contributions to musical theatre.

EARLY YEARS

Ball was born to an English father and a Welsh mother in Bromsgrove, Worcestershire. Initially aspiring to be an actor, his father Tony trained as an Austin apprentice at the Longbridge plant before rising to the position of head of global sales at British Leyland. He received an MBE for his contributions to the industry.

The maternal grandfather of Ball worked as a coal miner. Ball has two siblings: Katherine, who is over ten years Ball's junior, and Kevin, who is four years Ball's senior. When he was three years old, he and his parents relocated to Dartmoor.

He never had singing classes, but as a young boy, he picked up the skill through imitating songs by artists like Ella Fitzgerald, Mahalia Jackson, and Frank Sinatra. He enrolled in Plymouth College, an independent boarding school when he was 11 years old because his parents believed he would receive an excellent education there. He was upset about this, though, as he did not fit into the school's academic and extracurricular culture at the time. On Sunday morning, he did attend the Pathfinder bible study at St. Andrew's church

with his fellow junior boarders. He attended
Pathfinder camp on the island of Jersey one
summer.

Ball had a passion for the theatre, so
throughout the summer months, his father took
him to watch performances, including a King
Lear staged by the Royal Shakespeare Company
at the Royal Shakespeare Theatre, which had an
impression on him when he was around 14
years old. He participated in a youth theatre,
which led him to Guildford School of Acting,
where he discovered a setting that suited him.
He and a female student companion used to go
busking on Saturdays in Guildford town to

make a little more cash when they were students. His graduation was in 1984.

Ball's singing career took off right away after college. Ball's maternal grandmother was proud of his early singing accomplishments since she had a good ear for music; nevertheless, she passed away unexpectedly from a heart attack just a week before he made his stage debut in The Pirates of Penzance.

CAREER

Theatre

Ball's first role after graduating from drama school was in Godspell at the Aberystwyth Arts Centre in 1984. He then spent a few months working in rep in Basingstoke, but his big break came when he landed a lead role in The Pirates of Penzance at the Manchester Opera House. Ball was chosen at an open audition from about 600 applicants who lined up to participate in singing, acting, and dancing interviews that were conducted in three different rooms.

Cameron Mackintosh cast him as Marius in the original London production of Les Misérables, which was his next significant part. However, he had glandular fever and had to take six to seven weeks off work to recover from tonsillitis and the post-viral tiredness it brought with it. He was still exhausted when he got back to work, and he started experiencing on-stage panic attacks, which are characterised by intense anxiety, a quick heartbeat, perspiration, and eyesight issues. These also began to occur at other times, like as he was leaving for work. He lived alone in his flat for the majority of the following nine months, feeling miserable; he skipped counselling and quit Les Misérables.

Ball accepted an invitation from Thames Television to perform during the Miss England pageant, a live television event, and he did so successfully despite his anxiety. He later watched the film and was relieved to see that no one had noticed how scared he had been, so he was less concerned about his anxiety issue. When Michael Crawford, who played the Phantom, and Steve Barton, who played Raoul, left the London production to appear in the Broadway staging in New York City, Cameron Mackintosh asked Ball to play Raoul in the second casting of The Phantom of the Opera in London. Ball would not be under too much strain in the role of Raoul, in Mackintosh's opinion, and he is the appropriate actor for the role.

Ball portrayed Alex in the London and New York productions of Aspects of Love and Giorgio in the London production of Passion by Stephen Sondheim. His one-man show, Alone Together, was initially presented at the Donmar Warehouse (and then again in 2004 for the Haymarket's Singular Sensations season). Ball participated in three significant performances in 1998: Hey, Mr. Producer: The Musical World of Cameron Mackintosh (issued on CD and DVD), Sondheim Tonight at the Barbican Centre (published on CD), and The Fiftieth Birthday Concert of Andrew Lloyd Webber at the Royal Albert Hall (released on DVD). He was widely seen as having made a return when he played Caractacus Potts in the Sherman Brothers' musical Chitty Chitty Bang Bang in 2002.

He co-starred alongside Petula Clark in a 2004 Cork Opera House production of Lloyd Webber's Sunset Boulevard, which was subsequently televised by the BBC. Later that year, during Clark's Concert, which was also televised by the BBC, he performed as a guest. He sang "Home," "One Voice," and two duets with Clark from his most recent album, Since You've Been Gone, in addition to three other songs. Other appearances include singing at the BBC's St. David's Day event and playing Marius at the 1995 Les Misérables: The Dream Cast in an event concert, which celebrated the musical's tenth anniversary.

Ball, a lyric baritone, performed Les Misérables in a special concert for the Queen and her guests in 2004 at Windsor Castle, singing the part of Valjean. He took over for Michael Crawford, who had to leave the part of Count

Fosco in The Woman in White due to ill health, with 10 days' notice in 2005.

As Count Fosco in the Broadway transfer of The Woman in White from London's West End, Ball made a comeback to the stage in November 2005. However, he was forced to leave the show due to a viral infection that was allegedly brought on by the fat suit that was required for the part, and that caused Ball's body temperature to increase during the performance by several degrees.

Ball made his New York City Opera debut in the role of Reginald Bunthorne in Gilbert and

Sullivan's Patience in September 2005. Following the illness that forced him to leave The Woman in White on Broadway, he spent the first three months of 2006 on complete voice rest. Ball participated in The Rocky Horror Show's celebratory performance at the Royal Court Theatre by the middle of July. To promote his main part in Kismet for the ENO, he made an appearance on Richard & Judy on Channel 4 on June 22, 2007. Then, on August 27, 2007, at London's Royal Albert Hall, he made a contentious "Musical Theatre" Prom appearance as a solo artist for the BBC. Ball performed a variety of Andrew Lloyd Webber and other musical theatre songs. Both BBC

Radio 3 and BBC Four carried live broadcasts of the program.

Ball performed in the popular musical Hairspray at the Shaftesbury Theatre in London from October 2007 to July 2009, marking his comeback to the West End. He played Edna Turnblad. He received the Laurence Olivier Award for Best Actor in a Musical in March 2008 for his performance.

Additionally, for his performance as Edna Turnblad, he was given the Whatsonstage.com Theatregoers' Choice Award for Best Actor in a Musical.

He appeared alongside Imelda Staunton as Mrs. Lovett in a brand-new production of Sweeney Todd: The Demon Barber of Fleet Street at the Adelphi Theatre in the West End. The performance had its world premiere on September 24, 2011, at the Chichester Festival Theatre, and performed there for six weeks before moving to London in March 2012. For their performances in Sweeney Todd, Michaeléé, and Imelda received Olivier Awards for Best Actor and Best Actress in a Musical, respectively.

In the 2015 UK tour of Mack and Mabel, Ball played Mack.

In a staged concert performance of Les
Misérables, it was revealed in February 2019
that Ball will play Inspector Javert alongside
Alfie Boe (Jean Valjean). The musical will debut
on August 10, 2019, at the Gielgud Theatre and
act as a stand-in for Cameron Mackintosh's
new staging of Les Miserables at the newly
renamed Sondheim Theatre, which will take the
place of the show's original West End
production at the Queen's Theatre. On
December 2, 2019, the staged concert was
streamed live to theatres in the UK, followed by
encore presentations in both the UK and the
USA. The number of people watching this
staged concert live in theatres has reached an

all-time high in the UK. At the beginning of
2020, the live feed was also made available on
DVD and CD. On January 5, 2020, BBC Radio 2
broadcast the concert.

Ball returned to his role as Edna Turnblad in
the 2021 London Coliseum production of
Hairspray, which debuted on June 21.

Capturing Work

Ball is a concert performer who routinely travels throughout the UK and has also given performances in Australia and the US. He has achieved success with his recordings in the charts as well. Ball had less success with follow-up singles after penetrating the UK Singles Chart at No. 2 with 'Love Changes Everything' from Aspects of Love, but has primarily focused on releasing albums, all of which achieved gold status within weeks, and in the case of The Movies album in 1998, platinum status in seven weeks (released on October 26, confirmed platinum status on December 12).

Ball sang "One Step Out of Time," which placed second, as the UK's entry in the 1992 Eurovision Song Contest, which was held in Malmö, Sweden. The single peaked at number 20 in the UK, while the same year's self-titled album peaked at number 1. This started a string of top 20 albums that were released during the following 20 years. Ball performed as a guest on Julian Lloyd Webber's CD Unexpected Songs in July 2006, and that same year, in November, he also released a DVD of the best songs from his Live in Concert DVDs. Musicals, Love Songs, Personal Favourites, Party Time, and Unplugged are the five categories that make up this playlist. A brand-new "Unplugged" session that Ball specifically recorded in the studio with four other musicians was also included on the DVD. It was published on November 20th, 2006. Ball engaged in a lot of promotional events around the time his album One Voice was released towards the end of 2006. This featured performing the song "Home" on the Gloria Hunniford-hosted The Heaven and Earth Show on BBC One and GMTV on ITV.

In July 2007, a new compilation album by the name of Michael Ball: The Silver Collection as well as the DVD edition of his 1995 movie England My England were both made available.

Ball began work on his 15th solo album around the close of 2007, with plans to release it on October 15 of that same year. Back to Bacharach is the name of the album, which contains only songs that Burt Bacharach wrote. It was made available alongside the performance DVD of his One Voice Live 2007 tour, which was recorded at London's Hammersmith Apollo. For these releases, there were promotional events in October and November 2007 that included appearances on Friday Night with Jonathan Ross and Loose Women.

Ball's "Both Sides Now" CD, which includes the song "Fight the Fight" from Tim Rice's newest production From Here to Eternity, was released in February 2013.

Ball's album, If Everyone Was Listening, was made available in November 2014. He issued the album Coming Home To You in March 2019. Even though Ball has had numerous hits, this is his first solo album to achieve the top spot on the UK Albums Chart in 26 years.

With Alfie Boe, he has made three albums. Ball & Boe: Together in 2016 and Ball & Boe: Together Again in 2017 both peaked at number one. Ball & Boe: Back Together, their third album, peaked at number two on the UK Albums Chart in 2019.

Ball and Captain Tom Moore, a 99-year-old World War II veteran, collaborated on a duet in April 2020 to raise money for the NHS during the Covid-19 pandemic. On 24 April, their rendition of "You'll Never Walk Alone" peaked at the top of the UK Singles Chart, giving Ball his first number-one song at the age of 57 and making Moore the oldest person in history to have a number-one single.

Television

Ball made a brief acting appearance in Coronation Street in 1985 as Malcolm Nuttall. Ball has also dabbled in radio and television presenting. In 1993 and 1994, Ball had his TV show, Michael Ball. In 1995, he had a Christmas special, and in 1998, BBC Cymru Wales Ball in the Hall recorded a three-part series on him. To create the special that was then broadcast on BBC One, these three episodes were combined. The National Lottery Draws and Children in Need have both been presented by Ball. He briefly served as a guest presenter on This Morning.

In 2007, Ball co-judged the second season of the ITV reality program Soapstar Superstar. Ball spoke about his Welsh ancestry on the BBC Cymru Wales program Coming Home in 2010. He hosted 30 episodes of his own ITV daytime show, The Michael Ball Show, in 2010. Ball made six guest appearances on episodes of Lorraine on ITV Breakfast in 2010 and 2011.

Ball served as a substitute presenter for The One Show for the first time on April 10, 2013. Since then, he has performed as the show's host multiple times. After Paul O'Grady fell unwell, Ball appeared as a guest presenter on an

episode of the teatime talk show The Paul
O'Grady Show on November 18, 2013. He made
a cameo appearance as a fictionalised version of
himself in the British sitcom Toast of London
on November 24, 2013. Ball participated in a
celebrity-themed Christmas episode of
Catchphrase on December 29, 2013.

Diamonds are Forever: A Tribute to Don Black,
a special presentation honouring the
songwriter Don Black, was broadcast on BBC
Four on January 3 and was taped at London's
Royal Festival Hall. Ball performed two songs
on this program; the first was Born Free, which
was a smash for British male vocalist Matt

Monro in 1966 and won the Academy Award for Best Original Song. This song's lyrics were written by Black, and John Barry created the music for the Born Free movie. Love Changes Everything, which Black co-wrote with lyricist Charles Hart for the Andrew Lloyd Webber musical Aspects of Love, was the second song Ball sang throughout the show. Ball released this song as a single in 1989, and it spent fourteen weeks on the British pop charts. Ball was accompanied by the BBC Concert Orchestra for both songs in this performance.

Ball reunited with Imelda Staunton, his Sweeney Todd co-star, on December 26, 2014, when they both appeared in Victoria Wood's musical That Day We Sang.

Alfie Boe and Michael have co-hosted three ITV programs. The broadcasts took place in 2016, 2017, and 2019. Ball and Boe: One Night Only, 2016 2017: Ball and Boe Are Reunited 2019: A Very Merry Christmas from Ball and Boe.

Radio

Ball hosted several specials on topics like Cy Coleman, Nat King Cole, and Cameron Mackintosh as well as Ball over Broadway and The Greenroom on BBC Radio 2.

In 2008, Michael Ball's Sunday Brunch debuted on BBC Radio 2, taking Michael Parkinson's place after Parkinson's Sunday Supplement had terminated the year before. Up until September 2011, the program aired on Sundays between 11 a.m. and 1 p.m. It afterward shared its time slot with Weekend Wogan presented by Terry Wogan.

After a brief hiatus, Ball returned to Radio 2 in 2013 with a brand-new program called Sunday Night With Michael Ball, which aired on Sunday nights between 7 and 9 o'clock. On April 10, 2016, Ball returned to the Sunday morning time slot following the passing of Sir Terry Wogan, with the program now known as The Michael Ball Show. Later that month, Claudia Winkleman filled the vacant Sunday evening time slot.

Until 2016 on the station, he served as Ken Bruce's regular stand-in host.

MODERN CAREER

Ball began a lengthy tour of Britain in March and April 2007. The tour visited Wales, Scotland, Northern Ireland, and England on its 23 dates. Before a handful of performances in the north of England and the Midlands, the tour began with two nights in Belfast. After performing in Glasgow and Aberdeen, Ball travelled back to London, Birmingham, and Northampton. Before starting the last leg of his tour, Ball travelled to his former house in Plymouth. In addition to Ipswich and Northampton, Ball's trip also included Cardiff as its conclusion. After this tour, he made his operatic debut at the English National Opera in the title role of Hajj/Poet in a fresh staging of Robert Wright and George Forrest's Kismet.

With An Evening with Michael Ball at the Royal Albert Hall in August 2007, he made his BBC Proms debut—the first time a musical theatre performer has received a solo concert at the classical music festival.

On December 3, 2007, Ball sang "You Can't Stop the Beat" with the rest of the cast from the musical Hairspray at the Royal Variety Performance at the Empire Theatre in Liverpool. Up to April 29, 2009, he performed at the Shaftesbury Theatre in the musical Edna Turnblad.

On March 2, 2008, Ball made an appearance as a guest on the BBC Radio 4 program Desert Island Discs. During the interview, he discussed his upbringing, early career struggles with stage fright, and some aspects of his personal life. He gave several summer concerts, including one on June 14, 2008, at the Hampton Court Music Festival. Every Sunday from 11 a.m. to 1 p.m. starting on April 6, Ball takes over Michael Parkinson's Sunday Supplement on BBC Radio 2.

The Whatsonstage.com Theatregoers' Choice Award for Best Actor in a Musical was given to Ball in 2008. Additionally, he received his first Laurence Olivier Award in 2008 for Best Actor in a Musical.

The solo album Past and Present by Ball was made available by Universal Music on March 9, 2009. A collection of previously published songs honouring Ball's 25 years in the music business are included on the CD, along with six brand-new songs, including "You Can't Stop the Beat" from Hairspray. Ball made several appearances on radio and television shows to advertise the record. In the autumn, he celebrated his 25 years in the music business by touring the UK with an orchestra and five West End performers (Louise Clare Marshall, Louise Dearman, Emma Williams, Adrian Hansel, and Ben James-Ellis). A DVD of his performance at the Royal Albert Hall on September 19, 2009, was captured. On December 12, 2009, Ball participated in a "one-off" Christmas concert to support The Shooting Star Children's Hospice. This charity received all net earnings. Ball is a patron of the charity Shooting Star CHASE, which was formed in 2011 by the merger of the Shooting Star Children's Hospice and CHASE Hospice Care for Children.

Ball filled in as a substitute judge for Robin Cousins on ITV1's Dancing on Ice on February 14, 2010, when Cousins was in Vancouver for the Winter Olympics. The Michael Ball Show, a television pilot Ball recorded for ITV1 on February 10th, was picked up as a full series in the summer.

The O2 Arena hosted the Les Miserables 25th Anniversary Concert. Alfie Boe portrayed Jean Valjean, Norm Lewis played Javert, Lea Salonga portrayed Fantine, Ramin Karimloo played Enjolras, Hadley Fraser portrayed Grantaire, Katie Hall portrayed Cosette, Matt Lucas portrayed Thénardier, Jenny Galloway portrayed Madame Thénardier, Samantha Barks portrayed Éponine, and Nick Jonas portrayed Marius Pontmercy, the part Ball played in the original London production. An ensemble of 300 actors and musicians from the present London production, the international tour, and the original London production from 1985 participated.

Four Jean Valjeans sang "Bring Him Home" during the encore, including Colm Wilkinson from the original London cast, John Owen-Jones from the 25th Anniversary touring production, Simon Bowman from the current London cast, and Alfie Boe, who performed the part live. The group then performed "One Day

More" under the direction of the original 1985 cast. Students from Les Misérables school performances entered the arena to cap off the performance following remarks from Cameron Mackintosh, Alain Boublil, and Claude-Michel Schönberg. The evening concert was broadcast live to theatres in the UK, Ireland, and other countries. The 2010 broadcast was made available on Blu-ray and DVD in November 2010 in the UK and in February 2011 in North America.

The Olivier Awards were co-hosted by Ball and Imelda Staunton on March 13, 2011, at the Theatre Royal in Drury Lane, London. On

March 14, 2011, he released his album Heroes.

It debuted at position 10 on the UK charts.

Ball received an Honorary Doctorate of the Arts

from the University of Plymouth in 2013.

Along with Roger Moore, Stephen Fry, Ewan

McGregor, Joan Collins, Joanna Lumley,

Michael Caine, Charlotte Rampling, and Paul

McKenna, Ball supports the GivingTales app

for kids in 2017 to raise money for UNICEF.

The album debuted at the top of the UK

Albums Chart on March 29, 2019. Michael

Ball's fourth UK number-one album, Coming

Home to You, was his first solo number-one album since his self-titled first album in 1992. "It's the most thrilling news!" he said while speaking with the Official Charts Company. Thank you very much to the fans that connected with the album and purchased it for your support. This is merely the cherry on top after all of the hard work. Amazing!".

The Song "You'll Never Walk Alone"

Ball performed "You'll Never Walk Alone" live on BBC Breakfast in April 2020 to commemorate Captain Tom Moore's completion of the first leg of his fundraising walk during the COVID-19 pandemic at the age of 99. The performance was captured and turned into a digital single within 24 hours, using Moore's spoken words and the NHS Voices of Care Choir. The song was released by Decca Records with all earnings going to NHS Charities Together, and it immediately reached the top of the country's "The Official Big Top 40" chart. According to the Official Charts

Company, it was the "biggest trending song" and sold about 36,000 copies in its first 48 hours. Moore was the oldest person to hold that position when it reached No. 1 in the weekly "Official" UK Singles Chart on April 24. This means that he will be at No. 1 on his 100th birthday.

PRIVATE LIFE

Ball resides with Cathy McGowan, a former Ready Steady Go! presenter. They first connected in 1989 when she interviewed him during Aspects of Love rehearsals while working as an entertainment reporter for a BBC London magazine show. They've shared a home since 1992. She pulled him from an oncoming house fire on December 23, 2000, thus saving his life. Cathy had a daughter named Emma from her previous marriage to actor Hywel Bennett. Michael Ball's godson is Emma's son.

In April 2022, Ball returned to the Guildford School of Acting to address the class of graduating postgraduates. While he was there, Ball received an honorary doctorate from the University of Surrey.

Grace Crompton, a representative of England in rugby sevens and a 2022 Commonwealth Games participant, is Ball's step-granddaughter.

DISCOGRAPHY

Solo Albums

- Michael Ball (1992)

- Always (1993)

- One Careful Owner (1994)

- First Love (1995)

- The Musicals (1996)

- The Movies (1998)

- The Very Best of Michael Ball – In

  Concert at the Royal Albert Hall (1999)

- Christmas (1999 & 2000)

- This Time... It's Personal (2000)

- Centre Stage (2001)

- A Love Story (2003)
- Love Changes Everything – The Essential Michael Ball (2004)
- Music (2005)
- One Voice (2006)
- Back to Bacharach (2007)
- Past and Present: The Very Best of Michael Ball (2009)
- Heroes (2011)
- Both Sides Now (2013)
- If Everyone Was Listening (2014)
- Together with Alfie Boe (2016)
- Together Again with Alfie Boe (2017)
- Coming Home to You (2019)
- Back Together with Alfie Boe (2019)

- Together at Christmas with Alfie Boe (2020)
- We Are More Than One (2021)
- Together in Vegas with Alfie Boe (2022)

Cast Recordings

- Les Misérables – Original London Cast (1985) as Marius Pontmercy
- Les Misérables – Complete Symphonic Recording (1988) as Marius Pontmercy
- Rage of the Heart – Concept Album (1989) as Peter Abelard

- Aspects of Love – Original London Cast (1989) as Alex Dillingham
- West Side Story – Studio Cast (1993) as Tony
- Les Misérables – 10th Anniversary – The Dreamcast in Concert (1995) as Marius Pontmercy
- Passion – Original London Cast in Concert (1997) as Georgio
- Sondheim Tonight (1998) – Concert Cast
- Hey, Mr. Producer: The Musical World of Cameron Mackintosh (1998) – Concert Cast, Raoul in The Phantom of the Opera, Marius in Les Misérables

- Chitty Chitty Bang Bang – Original London Cast (2002) as Caractacus Potts
- Sweeney Todd: The Demon Barber of Fleet Street – London Revival Cast (2012) as Sweeney Todd
- Les Misérables – The Staged Concert (2019) as Javert

Other books written by this author include:

Alan Rickman: From Birth to Death of A Great Actor

Christian Bale: A Memoir Of The Most Adaptable Actor

George Harrison: Biography Of The Brilliant Beatles' Guitarist

Bruce Springsteen: Biography Of A Great Artist

Arnold Schwarzenegger: The Austrian Oak's Journey To Greatness

Patrick Stewart: Biography Of A Legendary Actor

Printed in Great Britain
by Amazon

30039677R00031